Call Me urple

Call Me urple

A RESTAURANT MANAGER'S STORY

JIM PARSONS

authorHOUSE®

AuthorHouse™ LLC
1663 Liberty Drive
Bloomington, IN 47403
www.authorhouse.com
Phone: 1-800-839-8640

Published by AuthorHouse   08/10/2013

ISBN: 978-1-4918-0698-2 (sc)
ISBN: 978-1-4918-0699-9 (e)

Library of Congress Control Number: 2013914407

Foreword

Writing this book has not been a labor of love or a desire to become independently wealthy, but simply a personal account of my years spent in the restaurant industry and my growth as a husband, father and fellow human being. The book's main theme is Diversity in all its forms. From the particular guests, employees, managers and all who will always be part of life's single pleasure, an escape from the daily grind of life of going out to eat. If this lifetime of journey can spark a memory or stir an emotion with in, or satiate a curiosity, then that is all the satisfaction I can hope for. All excerpts or flights of fancy in this book are not the opinions or practices of any corporation I worked for and only represent my personal observations and outlooks on this massive industry as a whole. Remember Life is about Diversity, Compromise and Acceptance in the spirit of this, just call me Purple.

Contents

Strutting and Fretting upon the Restaurant Stage

I am trying to sleep with everyone in this restaurant because my boyfriend cheated on me. This was one of the first employees I met at a quick service restaurant college internship. No, I did not sleep with her, but what an interesting journey I was about to embark on. The landscape of Restaurant Management is the basis for this story.

Overall it's been a hard and lonely road. The money is good, but the constant B.S. from guests, employees and upper management has made me question my work life a time or two. I will carry on through out this book covering interesting stories, observations of the industry and maybe some clarity on what happens when you go out to your favorite eatery.

Graduating from Purdue

Growing up in a "small town", sounds like a *Johnny Cougar* song, had given me very little references for what I was about to experience. Upon graduation from a Midwestern University, majoring in Restaurant Management, I accepted my first restaurant management position in a medium priced steak house. Newly married to my high school sweetheart, I lived in the parking lot where the restaurant was located, or actually the apartment complex was; three minutes to work.

The next six months of training would not begin to shed light on the road ahead. At 23, I was a very young manager. My first real education was when a young black dishwasher taught me sort the silverware after being ran through. That single act was the basis for my sense of urgency. I managed two twin ladies, Gay and Gina, I'll call them, in their middle 40's, they always fought over a single patron who tipped $50 no matter what; these were 1988 dollars mind you! We had his set table and chair to the back of the wall like Al Capone. The restaurant always stocked Moet White Star Champagne just for him. All in all he was the most generous customer I have ever seen. He bought Christmas hams for each staff member, including management. Thanks for the Dinner, he was no Scrooge.

Ah! Sir, I had an accident in the restroom, I'm sorry, she said at the hostess stand. Hey April, can you go get the busser and tell him to clean up the women's restroom. "Sure", Mr. Parsons, the mandatory address at the steak house. The busser returned to me and said he didn't know where to begin and would I take a look. As soon as I opened the door, the smell was as potent as a freshly laid pile of Doberman dog shit. As I approached the stall, I noticed a pair of soiled panties at the front of the toilet on the floor. Opening the door, I had been scared for life, hence this book of tales. There was shit all over the toilet, the floor, the back wall and both side walls. No 17 year old busboy was going to clean this up in five minutes with a mop. You can clearly see her bending over the throne to have her diarrhea explosion, however she missed like *Sammy Sosa* gong for the homerun record; she clearly exploded back and all around, before making that all important seat seal with her well-fed bottom. Forty minutes later, the bathroom was clean and I had my first story. I have never seen a mess like this one in the last twenty five years.

Jim with Kids at the Beach

My real goal in life was to move to the sunshine state, nine months out of college, I left the steakhouse and jumped into Florida with both feet. This is where Restaurant Management 101 was about to occur. I was now working in the Mall at an American bistro complete with Tiffany glass chandeliers, sounds fancy, huh! Don't be fooled, they did have a great salad bar though.

My first day I was introduced to three different people; Brother Dan, Daren and "Purple", or a Korean, a gay six foot six black bus boy and a white, no "Purple" cook. I found out that the Korean learned English by singing Christmas Carols 365 days a year. I can still hear, with his Asian accent, Jingle Bells Jingle Bells Jingle all the way, even on the fourth of July. I have carried his mantle all these years by randomly singing these songs to my staff whenever I needed a smile.

Hi Jim, my name is Daren, he stated, in his most gay, flame on voice, smiling down at me with his gold tooth ablaze; a six foot six gay black man. There was only one gay and one black in my whole high school, in the great Hoosier State. Nothing compares to meeting "Purple", a cook at this restaurant. You see, "Purple" had legally changed his name to "Purple" and he got permission from the corporate office to dye his clothes purple. He drove a purple car, he wore purple socks, purple underwear and his religion was purple. He believed in purple. Well, ok then. Welcome to crazy town. I'm not making this up. I managed another set of identical twins. The bartenders Georgi and Gavin were lady's men; bartenders by night and rock stars in the G.M.'s husband's band later at night. Coincidence with all four twins with their names starting with G, I think not!

There were three things that stood out to me at this mall food outlet. The first of the three was when my boss asked me to ask a male flasher to leave the restaurant after he had cut out the crotch in his pants then opened his legs to the ladies across from him. I walked up and said sir, I'm afraid you will have to leave. His reply, No problem, like it was another episode of Jeopardy and Alex Trebek said his answer was incorrect. The second was when the G.M. had noticed, one night, that someone had crawled up into the ceiling via a displaced ceiling tile in the men's restroom. She demanded the wiry short bartender go up and find this peeping Tom, probably over the lady's restroom. He did as told and a few minutes later came crashing down through the ceiling onto two families finishing dinner. Glad I didn't have to handle this one. No one was ever found. The next Hollywood tale is just that. I have never seen a movie influence the masses or pop culture like "Batman"; you know the Michael Keaton/Jack Nicholson version. We routinely got blasted from the movie theater plex across the hall. The head cook was so excited he carved a watermelon into a bat and hung it from the top of the salad bar. We served joker cocktails in the bar all throughout the run of the film.

Getting transferred after 1.5 years to the middle of the Sunshine State was not my plan, but probably good for my career. It was time for some sweet Coco. Coco was a manager at the new location and looked like Dolly Parton in every possible way, sorry honey. Every day I was here we would talk about her boobs because she would always bring them up. She said they always met somebody before she did! I'm sure that is the way the affair started with the married G.M. While he was harassing her, I was getting harassed by Karen; her antics included standing in the middle of the kitchen alley with her skirt pulled high wearing a thong as I walked through the kitchen door. She asked me to sleep with her and I said No, I explained I was married and no thank you. She went to the G.M. and explained her concern with my response. The G.M. confronted me and said I needed to learn how to play the game. I was confused and said she needed to stop. We clearly did not see eye to eye. Karen would remain mad and later I would have two of the lesbians confront and grope me in the office, concerning Karen. Don't worry, I'm not that prudish, but was trying to remain faithful to my wife.

The bar was busy and I was in charge of increasing alcohol sales. I decided to put a paper bag on a bottle of Licor 43; a vanilla liquor that had been in the restaurant for three years since the opening. I wrote "unknown shot" on the bag vertically; three dollars was the price. We sold it in a day and a half. Don't worry, we added a fruity mixer.

Jim as the Flash

Hey, I'm pretty good at this marketing thing. As Halloween approaches, I plan to distribute candy to mall passersby. Why not in costume, not Batman, but the Flash was the latest live action TV series on. They said I was a fat flash. Oh well and why not a pumpkin, so I took the head cook's idea and my uncle's present of a food garnishing book and carved my first restaurant logo pumpkin.

Caged Pumpkin

I would later win the Conner Prairie pumpkin carving contest three years in a row. Being interviewed by local news TV, and having my face and pumpkin in the paper, I was the "Prince of Pumpkins". My first born child was born on October 12th, you see, October was a very big month for me.

You may be wondering how many hours you have to work in this industry. It ain't no nine to five job. The first restaurant I worked, six days for three weeks and got off two days in a row once a month. The current restaurant is five, twelve hours shifts per week plus meetings and inventories on my days off. It sure beats the hours *William Shatner* had to spend on the set filming Star Trek. Of course, he will probably sell more books than I will.

Now is the time to move, "Back Home Again in Indiana", sorry for the song title usage, Jim Nabors. My wife wanted to have family around for our first born.

It takes a village or a region to make a restaurant successful. Same company, but different unit number four, was like night and day. Same menu, but poor leadership forced me to consider other vocational options, like used car salesman. Holy cow! My boss graduated from the same college I did. "Draw" partner that is how I survived with no benefits and roller coaster income. I was proud to have the highest gross at the dealership for a single car sell, I wonder if it still stands. All I know is they cut me a check for $2000; I wonder what they made.

The most blatant sexual harassment did not occur in the restaurant, but here in the sales manager's office at the dealership. Bryce, the sales manager had all the salesmen in his office laughing and joking when Sherry, a college intern, walked by the office in the hall and the room goes silent. Bryce sits back in his big leather chair behind the sales desk and says, Sherry, you have perfect legs. Sherry says what? He retorts, you have perfect legs. Sherry says, what are you talking about? He said, you know, feet on the bottom and pussy on the top. The whole room was silent; Sherry says nothing and walks away; College Intern "1" third year sales manager "0". The next day, he was clearing out his desk. According to the wisdom of *Donald Trump,* YOU ARE FIRED!

Six months and I was back in the game. That's right, a five to six day work week; every other week six days, but only ten hour shifts. Nothing has changed, bra parties after hours in the restaurant, another holiday pumpkin display and a manager sleeping his way throughout the staff. Having an informant that the Playmate of the Year was coming to dinner was magical. I rushed to the newsstand and bought five copies of the current issue of Playboy and had her sign them for all the managers plus a photo of her and me in the lobby of the restaurant. Ladies and Gentlemen, I present to you *"Miss Corinna Harney".* She is at the table with *Chevy Chase* in "Vegas Vacation" when he asked her if she was a pro. She declined and walked away. At least I got a picture, Chevy.

Employees I can trust

It's time for a Christmas "Karol" and I don't mean that Korean singing a song. A server named Karol was a particular sort who gave the universal greeting to men folk more times than I can count. That's right; she would grab their junk for shock value and even grabbed the Area Manager in the kitchen alley. I guess I did learn how to play the game. She grabbed me a time or two. Don't worry, my wife knows this.

Why have you never slept with anyone else, as if to indicate this was a perk for all restaurant managers. I simply stated to the hot bartender in the same restaurant that it was all just warm and wet and I was on a role. Why spoil it. She promised that it was not the same and she would rock my world, like *Gene Simmons* at a *Kiss* concert spitting blood and fire in an orgasmic end to "Lick it Up".

Opening of a new store, I am promoted to First Assistant, just like *Will Riker;* it was time for *The Next Generation.* However, I still got a shitty job, no, not a cleanup in the bathroom. I had to fire an eighty year old man. The boss had hired his friend to host, but he could not remember which tables to seat the guests. So my boss pussed out and made me call the grim reaper. As he was crying, I felt my heart go black and cold, I remembered what my father had told me, "people fire themselves; I have never fired anyone in twenty-five years".

The Orient Express is Coming Round the Bend

I took another break from the restaurant business and put tires on axles for an Indiana Trailer Company. But the Orient was calling or at least a new Chinese Restaurant chain. After twelve weeks of training and two months as kitchen manager, I was promoted to General Manager. Shay Shay Nee, that is Chinese for thank you. Do you want to know how an Asian tells another Asian apart? They have to ask each other because they all look alike. This excerpt came from my Asian managers. This was my favorite restaurant of all to manage; however, this was like going from the human carnal buffet over the last few years, to a strict code of morality and reverence. Having taken a course in Asian sensitivity, as required by my company, I was now up to the task. "Purple" would have been proud. The days were normal and I even had the President come in and have lunch with me and asked me how to improve our sixty unit chain. Wow! Two presidents in two chains; I must be special. Don't worry, after the next restaurant I never saw another president in my unit again, no tears were shed.

Remember, The Guest is Always the Guest

By now you are probably wondering what bullshit I had to endure as stated at the beginning of my tale. Starting with the guest, remember the guest comes first or the guest is always right. Well, if you want your weekly pay check, you have to become immune to all comments, threats and sometimes physical violence; yes, I still have a mortgage. At twenty-three, I had to break up two guests threatening to come to blows. One was 6'5, drunk and mad at the lesser man, 5'6 and queer as a three dollar bill. With my big boy pants and calm demeanor, I came between the two and calmed oh skyscraper down and requested he return another day as I valued him as a guest, NOT! I did all of this knowing earlier Mr. Three dollar Bill had slapped my hand abruptly for removing what seemed to be an empty scotch glass. He then retorted after the whack, "Always ask before removing anything" as he sucked the last bit of the *Johnny Walker* out of the single ice cube that was left. A lesson I never forgot, always protecting my digits and pride.

A couple of years later, my managers had warned me about a certain family, not unlike the *Kardashians,* let their rat like offspring run through the dining room while they were in hot pursuit with *Bud Light* bottles in hand. I decided enough was enough and did not care about corporate support. This was my restaurant damn it! HEY, in a loud thunderous voice above all others, I stated, the couple froze and looked like two puppies about to be whipped for peeing in the house again. With absolutely no manager tact or scripted lines from the "one minute manager", I truly treated them like a guest in my home. I told them this was unacceptable and crazy. This was my restaurant and they would have to leave and take their children and not return. After pointing out the spilled beer from their bottles and the disgust from other patrons watching the show, they tucked their tails and granted my wish like a Genie from the bottle. Of course, there was an ovation from the other guests and no call to the Corporate. The same guests even returned next week like perfect customers. Maybe they were into domination; I did not care as long as it was a peaceful shift.

The restaurant industry has done it to itself. Having literally given away thousands of dollars from the house over the last twenty-five years, some of which as if the guests held a gun to my head and stole their dinners just for fun or to see if they could. Overcooked steaks, slow service, dirty silverware, rude employees or a particular 10 oz cut of salmon as gorgeous as *Marilyn Monroe,* but unacceptable because it was not a center cut from the loin. Well I guess Ethiopia will continue to starve at an alarming rate. This dinner is going in the trash and I have to buy the next one. But no I didn't. Like clockwork there was a call to corporate and $60 was sent out to the guest even though he said I apologized and no where in the menu does it state the type of cut, only 10 oz guaranteed. We didn't' even spit or put any other bodily type of fluids in his replacement dinner, like the movie "Waiting" suggested. *Jack Daniels* stock went up one time because a patron said his Jack on the rocks contained, no *Jack Daniels.* High time to get involved; I poured his drink from the opened bottle at the bar in front of him, but no, this was still considered to be a fake. I know I got him this time. I pulled a fresh, unopened bottle carefully removing the housing and opening the top as sure as it was a security sealed bottle of *Tylenol.* Epic Fail. He literally sat there and said this was no *Jack Daniels.* A valuable lesson was learned, the guest is truly not always right, but sometimes there is no way to please or win back. Know when to say "Have a Nice Day".

Down the road, in a restaurant not so far away, I had a guest recovery opportunity that I still think about today. May I speak to the G.M. please, we have been out of town for three months and we had a poor dining experience for all four of us and wonder if you cold comp our dinners next time we are in. Seriously, over ninety days ago and just now you are calling, is forefront in my head. Hey, I want a refund for the Colts/Saints Super bowl, my team didn't win. She explained her poor dining experience to me and without even doing the due diligence of looking up her check, server and verification. You know all corporate restaurants can do this fairly easily. I said, there was a time limit on complaint resolution. But I was truly sorry and will do better in the future. A few minutes later, a gentleman called and stated he was a car salesman and his wife had just called. He said that I had lost his business forever. Reprimanded me and down playing my assumed low salary, you know restaurant managers are usually paid fairly well plus receive a quarterly bonus. He said he would do anything to keep a customer or make a sale. No he did not call corporate. Gee, should I have given him the gift card? You be the judge; I still have to live with it.

Regular guests are in no short supply, but one lady takes the enchilada. "Como Estas?" How are you in Spanish was the theme for the next corporate restaurant. Kim came in 363 days a year, ordering the same lunch, with chips extra dark, sitting in the same special chair at her own table, ten minutes before we opened everyday. Taking two sips out of her soda and having it replaced because it was no longer fresh, never once trying anything else. She was there and saw more than I did and I was the G.M. Talk about consistent *Howie Mandel* behavior. The only reason it was not 365 days was because we were closed on Thanksgiving and Christmas. Sorry to say I carved no pumpkin for this store. Purple and Kim would've gotten along swimmingly, because of their individual obsessions. Diversity makes the world go 'round as well as keep giving me a paycheck as long as I accept it.

Great Employees are Hard to Come By

My career has been in no short supply of great employees and memorable ones. A bartender who was an ex Georgia championship wrestler, said she wanted to swallow my manhood and yearned for a facial. Wow, thirty-eight years old and I still have it, or not. I never took her up on it. At the same place, I had an all staff meeting and recognized the success we had in this turn around store. The bet from upper management was, I would not last six months-max, I later found out. But in the three years I was there as the Captain of the ship, I could not contain myself and cried like a baby giving the highest compliments to the managers and staff when we had won two awards for the best store in the Midwest region, two years in a row.

Twenty five years seams like a long time, but does not compare to the server I knew who opened a unit of the largest Italian restaurant in the world, in 1983. Breadsticks anyone? I just visited her in the summer of 2012 and she is going into management. Wow, 30 years of all you can eat breadsticks; she was consistently amazing. Amanda, thanks for the memories.

Ola, Seniorita! This server had more regulars than I have ever seen, bar none. They would even wait for her on their lunch break, just to have Juanita wait on them. If that was not impressive enough, when she went on vacation, they would boycott the restaurant; our sales actually dropped. Nobody served chips and salsa like Juanita.

Jim on Sailboat

In true fashion, I must thank some managers that I have worked with over the years. Thanks for taking me sailing on your eight person boat in the Gulf of Mexico, Thanks for taking me to that men's club and buying the lap dance from a server from my first restaurant a couple of years earlier. Thanks for inviting me to your amazing wedding and presenting me a statue of *Mel Gibson* as *Braveheart* from your Emerald isle honeymoon. Thanks for promoting me to G.M. for the first time, even though the Orient Express was derailed and decommissioned. Thanks for not walking out when we had no bartender, no host, no busser and only three servers on Saturday night; only going on a false wait for three hours straight. Thanks for not firing me when our Mother's Day was a disaster and all meals took over an hour to get out of the kitchen for six hours straight and I was the K.M. Thanks for awarding me "the best restaurant in the region" for a second time, when others did not agree, I thought it was our best year. I still have the gas grill you bought for me. Thanks for letting me work in Florida; I will retire there in five or six years. And finally, A big thanks to the industry for never letting me go hungry. You bought me 6,525 meals and still going strong. I need to go on a diet, oh, wait a minute, I am on one.

The Dark Side of the Industry

A true account of this industry would not be complete unless I shared with you the temptations, pitfalls and yes even the black hole of routine dishonesty it creates. Being an educated man and having taken the same safe food safety exam eight separate times passing it with flying colors I assure you the "5" second rule does exist. Don't be naïve and think anyone would throw away a 20 oz porterhouse just because it falls on the floor or a hamburger as it falls into the grease trough along side the grill at your favorite quick service burger joint. I have worked with hundred of employees and managers over a quarter of a century and there is not one honest Abe among the bunch. Most of what I saw amounted to no more than routine speeding an acceptable crime in this country or at least until you get pulled over. The industry puts strict guidelines on food and labor cost controls to make sure there is enough money for the President's new leather chair. This is where the never ending abyss of daily corruption begins. Ever wonder why a restaurant sits half empty but asks you to wait as the manager explains that they are busier than usual or they are short staffed? Ninety-nine percent of the time, this is a well crafted lie; like squeezing lemons for more fresh lemonade. The corporate won't allow the operator to staff the restaurant with people who only make $ 2.13 an hour. Don't clock in until you get your first table or hurry up and clock out, forget about that necessary cleaning duty. I wonder if Wal-Mart or the local chain grocery store operates like this with having only two check lines open but having 10-20 checkout lines available. If it is not clear by now, most kitchens are run by a Hispanic crew. The very people we are trying to send back over the border but can't because your $ 10.00 burger would cost you $ 50.00 if we gave the cooks an appropriate living wage, like a UAW worker who ultimately forced the government bailout and "cash for clunkers program", a car dealership rejuvenation bill. Cutting employee hours, rolling back the clocked in hours after the employee is long gone. You know we can't have any overtime. Portion control on food is the corporate staple for consistent profitability, but just like *Sam the butcher* on *The Brady Bunch,* pushing his thumb down on the deli scale. Hey less is more, more for the business or manager going for a hefty quarterly bonus. Although let me go on record to say, I have never made a great bonus. The best I ever got was $ 2300.00 from one quarter, usually making $ 5000.00 take home for the year in bonus. Not the pot of gold the corporate says is at the end of the rainbow. Some managers have made well over $10,000, not in a year, but for several quarters straight. Was it luck or hard work, or were they speeding through the industry and never got pulled over? One manager left me with $ 17,000.00 in unpaid repair bills. My unit had to pay for the damage done, making my store bonus ineligible for the whole year. And yet, another manager stole three store daily deposits, was not prosecuted and was even paid his salary and bonus to avoid litigation. Again, my store paid for poor judgment of the previous leader.

In this day and age, 1-800 how is my driving is the measure of performance in my industry. The days of comment cards are gone. Computers have provided instant feed-back even while you are still in the restaurant and have created a conflict free way to criticize or over criticize with out coming face to face with the one person who can help them, the manager. Instead the corporate expects perfect scores every time, but wait a minute, are we not told we can always improve, so how can we give a perfect score.

Health inspections come usually twice a year like clockwork and internal inspections are like a horse and pony show. It's next to impossible to control human behavior drinking, eating or picking your nose at wrong time will end your perfect score dream. Kitchens are hot and there is not time to do anything but cook. Is it too much to ask for some water, more often then not, I have rarely eaten or gone to the bathroom, a typical 10-12 hour shift. Try telling that to the worker at Chrysler or a member of the teamsters.

If you are a server working in the business it's like working in Las Vegas, you never know what kind of tip you will get. Tip is too insure prompt service. An 18% tip is the going rate. Once again, if the industry paid the server a solid salary you couldn't afford to eat out and it would go back to cooking and cleaning for ourselves like before the restaurant explosion occurred in this country.

I once saw a server get a $ 357.00 tip on a table of 3 and even her knees were still clean. The next day the same guest gave her $ 170.00 with no ulterior motives. He was flashing money for his guests.

Server theft has always been present from famous coupon scams. You go buy 20 copies of the Sunday paper and then use the $ 5.00 off two entrée coupon after people have paid their bill before closing the check, a quick $ 100.00 for a $ 10 or a $ 20 dollar investment. The tip switch is on the increase servers often change tips and when Managers do not follow up, it can cost you your reputation and you will lose guests.

Bartenders have been notorious for not ringing in drinks and pocketing cash or watering down the booze or even bringing in their own liquor so as not to red flag the restaurants inventory. The temptation for free booze is always great. A server once "fired himself", as my dad would say, for pouring Jack Daniels into a cartoon designed kids cup and was caught red handed by the manager and bartender. His response, "oops, I did not think I would get caught". The Busser once put a cooked ham into the garbage and upon the nightly trash run, he proceeded to "fire himself" when discovered. A cook openly was drinking a bottle of Bud Light on the back dock and remarked, "Oh Well, I guess I'm done". Everyone sneaks a French fry, a packet of crackers or a star light mint. Whether they are allowed or not this is the dilemma of self entitlement.

A Personal Sacrifice

Half the USA is employed in the hospitality field. There are thousands of restaurants in the U.S. and the World. What they don't tell you in college is that you give up all these holidays that you took for granted in elementary, middle and high school. OK, maybe they do, but I have missed seeing my mom for 25 straight Mother's days and counting. I am not crying though to keep the roof over head and clothes on their back, my family has learned to compromise and never wondering where daddy was on Christmas Eve or the highly anticipated 4th of July Celebration.

My family has helped over the years in my staffs' morale, repair and maintenance of my restaurants, local store marketing guest count increase and corporate image representation of my current flavor of the year. Let me say, Thanks to my wife and three children. An example of this was my children for several years have helped by wrapping holiday presents for my entire units' staff, not knowing they were giving their old man bonus points on his review that would help out at promotion time, allowing him to buy G.I. Joe with the Kung Fu Grip for their own Christmas enjoyment.

Early on my wife was bored at home and had helped closing my restaurant by filling out paperwork or counting the day's take for deposit, so I could get home quicker. This was later frowned upon by the G.M. Hey, it's easier to ask for forgiveness than permission!

My son would earn free lunch for picking up the parking lot or basic landscaping duties a few times. My daughter even painted a portrait of three servers holding liquor bottles that was presented to the group at an alcohol sales awareness meeting. One of these girls in the portrait is a new manager for the same company.

Restaurant Speak

Terminology in this industry is similar to the made up language of *Klingon* in the *Star Trek* Universe. Using code words, for people, processes, food, objects and guest relations. "Behind You", "Hot!" "Coming Through!" is an effort to create a safe environment just like a submarine in close quarters. "Down ladder make a whole". "86 this and that", if it's A-1 sauce you can expect a call to corporate. Oh wait a minute, this really did happen once. I "86'd" breadsticks once, that's like no shakes at *Steak and Shake*. Ordering food for sale in the business seems easier than it is. In 25 years I have never worked for a restaurant that we did not run out of food from time to time, but how about for a whole year. One restaurant changed their meals end offering from Andes mints to Breath Savers. No kidding the guests were so upset they even had a plane sky write over the corporate headquarters, "Bring Back Ande's Mints!". No, I did not get a kick back from Ande's. Monkey dishes, ramekins, fajita condoms, nuke it, love sauce, sticks, rarebits, luckys, or run it through the garden are names for food, equipment or cooking processes. There are also words to describe people as well. As much as I like Michael J. Fox or William Shatner when we speak of Canadians, we are not referring to our Northern neighbors. This is a code word for African Americans, you know black people, the old school word. The word Canadians is so prevalent that some human resource departments have sent memos to their restaurants prohibiting its use in employee descriptions of its patrons. One manager I know even got reprimanded for whistling a version of the scarecrow's song from *The Wizard of Oz* "If I only had a brain", when a server would make a mistake.

Advertising In Song

Jim in paper as Prince of Pumpkins

The restaurant business has kept my creative fires burning, you already knew me as the "Prince of Pumpkins", but never forget I was Jim Parsons before *Sheldon* from *The Big Bang Theory* was Jim Parsons. Which means I was strutting and Fretting on the game board of life, even wearing my Flash Costume at the restaurant long before he ever thought to do so. Not a stranger to showmanship, I performed in my high school's show choir.

Jim and Family at Follies

This would lead me and my entire family to perform in the local High school's Fund Raiser Musical Follies. My restaurant agreed to sponsor one of the many commercials that were traditionally put to song through a popular chorus. The city's Sheriff was a regular voice in the Follies and alongside the long arm of the law we sung our way to first place in this musical extravaganza. I hope no one was "too crabby" about this. We were also granted an award for "family making it family"; Thanks to the Parsons "5".

Jim with Merlin in Camelot

    This would not be the last time I marketed the restaurant through song. My restaurant would sponsor a local theater production of "Camelot". Playing Sir Sagramore and other melodious roles, I was able to sing my way to the cast party celebrating the director's first production at my restaurant. The night was wonderful and created loyal new guests at my restaurant. I have often spoken of doing dinner theater many times after I retire from the industry. I just won't be cooking, serving or cleaning up any more. Thank you I will be here all night. I never knew how hard it would be to jump to the canvas of words on a page medium for my artistic outlet, my hand is killing me.

My Favorite Restaurants

    Are you a local or regular at an established eatery? I have to say I am not. I like a varied, buffet, but I have had my favorites. I remember from my childhood, a Florida Seafood house, simply amazing; the server even looked like Clark Kent, you know the *Christopher Reeve* version. I remember a corporate Christmas dinner the $ 50.00 steak melted in my mouth, best I ever had. We have had family celebrations and get-togethers. A unique time was my wife's and my wedding rehearsal dinner that we had in the local restaurant and years later in the same banquet room but a different restaurant now; we celebrated my Mom and Dad's 50th Wedding Anniversary. If the walls could only talk.

My wife, three kids and I ate at the Rio Carnival Buffet in Las Vegas; the largest buffet that I have ever seen. I have been to Fondue restaurants, Brazilian style and black tie affairs, 5 Star services eateries and not to mention corporate banquets almost coast to coast. To reenergize each restaurateur's Management style. We celebrated my Mom's 70th Birthday at a restaurant I was a General Manager years before.

Famous People

I have seen many famous people in the places over the years visiting my friend in Long beach, California; I ate in his hotel, roof-top restaurant, you know where *Arnold Schwarzenegger* filmed "Last Action Hero", No, Arnold was not there, but *Perry Mason (Raymond Burr)* walked by my table. I actually met "William Zabka" you know, the original *Karate Kid's* Nemesis; Johnny, at a night club on spring break in Florida. A personal hero actually ate in two different restaurants I managed. *Tom Zupanzic;" the strongest neck in the world",* as stated by Guinness. I talked with Tom and caught up for a bit; what a nice guy. Mickey Gilley and his band came by for a quick bite to eat at a store, under my watch. A local grocery store Icon, a playmate of the year, a slew of local newscasters and local sports heroes have dined in my presence. You know everyone has to eat and everyone's money spends the same. I enjoyed a few visits with *Robert Mathis*, defensive linebacker for *the Indianapolis Colts.* We discussed his bench press weight and my goals at

47. I nailed 315 in an old man contest while Robert's is over 400. Still, it has kept me in shape for this fast-paced industry.

Jim sitting on Bench going for 335 lb bench-press

My Start in the Industry

When I was twelve, I recall my neighbor, who lived down the street with his big house and in-ground pool, owned a local pizza franchise and did quite well. My Mother always was willing to show me cooking secrets and encouraged me to help with the family dinner. I've told this next story so many times it might even be "true", to quote *Stan Lee*. No, but seriously, I really did live in Gallipolis, Ohio right down the hill from Bob Evans. I even went swimming in his pool once and went to the Bob Evans Farm Festival to watch my mom perform in a show girl review. Well, the Show must go on. Being a rich kid "Not" as my kids point out, my parents were members of the local country club. Working in the kitchen was the beginning for my interest in the industry though I never did remove the family of bats living in the chimney as the club manager requested. Come on let's save the club money, I say, let's call Orkin! The Colonel provided my first start in a corporate restaurant. This was my daughter's first job as well; coincidence, I think not.

Restaurant Etiquette

For years, I have wanted to write a book about going out to eat and how to behave and what to expect; they never had this course in high school or even college. Well, here goes: To start have enough money to pay your bill, I have sob stories on lost wallets, and "I know my credit card should work, I just made a payment", or people want to join the "dine and dash club" like it is not a crime or something. Server's work for $ 2.13 an hour in most of the country: tipping is expected at 18% on the total of the bill and if you want separate checks, be prepared to wait. Imagine, each transaction is separate and you are not the only table they have. Remember the meal should be hot and taste good, but not the first Ferrari off the line with leather bucket seats; it's just one meal. If your steak is off one temp, "shut your pie hole" and just eat it. The more you modify the more the cost, time or chance of mistake. Kids are meant to be seen; not heard. Enough said. Help keep your table clean, some people think it's a food fight like in "Animal House". Don't use profanity to make a point, "damn it!" Remember, if you have a legitimate complaint for the service, ask for a manager while you are there; don't call back later because this says you didn't want the problem fixed, you just want free food. Tag, you're it! It's not rude to show your coupon up front, Bravo! This helps your server ring in your order. Speaking of which, if you are in a large party, this will take a while, especially with a lot of modifiers. Contrary to the corporate goals, drinks from the bar and orders from the kitchen don't always take the same amount of time, please be patient. You want the truth? Never eat out when you are in a hurry, have to be at the movie or have somewhere else to be. There are no guarantees you are going to get your food on time. Ordering well done food takes longer, obviously. Ultimate stress free dining revolves around no time considerations and no over inflated expectations of the food or service. I will never eat out on Sundays. The managers are the newest, as well as the staff and they are exhausted from Friday and Saturday nights, probably, as well. Avoid restaurant closing in 30 minutes. Every one wants to leave; the food is old, cold and not as fresh. Go ahead and bring a bullet for yourself if you walk in at five minutes till closing. Everyone else already has the gun. I have had tables stay three hours after closing, while not paying their bill, forcing the restaurant from doing its paperwork and final clean up. Trust me, the restaurant chain doesn't even want you there, you cost them money and possible employee turnover, if this happens too often. Know how to drink socially, don't force me to intervene, even though I have asshole training, do you really want me to make you feel like a screw-up or inadequate human being? DWI does not stand for Dance Winner Inside. Be nice to people, make eye contact, never begrudge someone who handles your food, you never know when you will get more than you bargained for.

Pour me Some Alcohol

Having never consumed a bottle of beer, glass of wine or a cocktail of any kind, which includes 4 years on the same floor at the same university where kegs were commonly rolled in or out. I have tasted more than most people will ever know exist. My mom calls me the preacher of the family; however, I have seen too much tragedy that comes in a bottle. Its 5:00 somewhere, like Jimmy Buffet says, time to head down to Margaritaville. A choice beverage among the serious is green chartreuse; shots of this will put hair on your chest ladies, or maybe it's time for "the unknown shot". You know, a standard keg of beer in most restaurants weighs 155 lbs; I carried this by myself up two flights of stairs once, so someone could have a nice frosty glass of draft. Don't tell my doctor. Overtime and places worked, people like different concoctions. One place made a drink called a Tie Dye, which had four different frozen layers and a jellybean floating; four different liquors for a rainbow effect. I tasted 30 wines at Walter Payton's Roundhouse in Chicago, one paired chocolate and potato chips surprisingly they went well. Rule of thumb is: any wine that you want with any meat is the right choice. I once pointed out to my parents in an upscale, 5 star restaurant, how the bottle of Louis XIII sparkled on the shelf and they could see the bartender pull it down for $ 100.00 per shot. Yes, a Benjamin Franklin just like the one in the swimming pool from "Tower Heist" where even a clip of my University's Band can be seen. When I was younger, I received gasoline alley credentials from my Budweiser rep, had my picture taken with Bud girls and Clydesdales at the Indy 500 and all the beer I could drink. I still have to apologize to my brother for not enjoying that day to the fullest. I have seen light up glasses, trays and ice cubes, nothing compared to Formula One Race out at the track. I purchased light up Indy style key chains, hung them on a straw and made a frozen concoction that looked like the Italian Flag. I sold over 200 in two days; I called it the Frozen F1, Michael Schumacher would have been proud. That put me on the top alcohol sales list for the month in my region.

Jim with Bud Girls

I'm Not a Chef But . . .

In order to be called a chef you need a degree in Culinary Arts. I have managed American, Italian, Mexican, Chinese, Steak and Seafood Restaurants. I have picked up a thing or a thousand in food preparation styles and recipes from well over 15 corporate chefs, plus one pastry chef who cooked in the Whitehouse on the Residential side for Bill Clinton and his First Family.

It's hard to say which food I like best, but like most Americans, I love pizza and have driven for over two hours to Old Chicago just to savor their tasty pie. Cilantro is one of my favorite herbs and I love roasted red peppers. I recently discovered a Thai Peanut Sauce that is delicious; you should try it some time to spice up your poultry, it is in the Asian food section at the grocery store.

I'm not a huge seafood fan, but I love good fried shrimp or shrimp cocktail. One of the benefits of working in the kitchens for so long, I memorize the recipes making it easy to duplicate their famous Alfredo sauce, guacamole, French onion soup or General Tso's Chicken. Wok cooking is an art. I was proud when I made Egg Foo Young correctly on the first try in front of my Asian Chef Instructor. No, it did not blow apart in the wok. I have learned how to smoke and roast ribs; beef and pork competing with my friend Julie Parks, along time step aerobics partner, and successful restaurant owner of "Parky's Smokehouse". No charge for the free advertising, Julie, but if you want to buy my dinner, Oh Well!

Opening my Own Restaurant

Ok, at this point, you are saying this guy has been around the restaurant block so open up your own place already. But wait, a minute, restaurants go out of business everyday and I have been involved with or personally closed twelve different eateries. Whether my job hopping was beneficial or not to my career it would have been necessary at the end of the buffet line. It takes money; hey I'm a struggling writer like "James Joyce" who died drunk and penniless. People you can trust these days are in short supply. As my family would tell you I have not embraced technology. Heck, I have never sent a text message in my life, OMG! LOL. I want to be accessible but not that accessible. I don't even know my emergency soap dish phone number. No, you can't have it.

So you Want to be a
Restaurant Manager

My intention for this book was to also be guide to all those thinking about a career in the restaurant business, either corporate or private and the diversity of daily, weekly, monthly and yearly obligations.

Set yourself up for success. Eat right, sleep right, and get plenty of exercise. This is not bad advice from "Dr. Jim". I go through ten articles of clothing a day that's 50 pieces, on a five day work week and ten or more on days off; an average of 75 pieces a week, that's 300 a month. Thanks to my loving wife, I have never done laundry. But she has never once picked up an iron. My clothes are always wrinkle-free to impress peers and bosses. Pick up a bottle of wrinkle release, or make your own out of fabric softener. Establish your daily ritual, pick out your garanimals for the next day before you hit the hay, spray them down, hint dry by morning. Have all your keys, notes, wallet, watch and charged phone ready to go everyday. Make sure your alarm is working and you can hear it. Hey, I have over-slept before, but have only been late to work twice in 25 years: once due to an ice storm that virtually shut down all roads to work and once because both my cars broke down trying to get me to the "church" on time. I always quote this motto, "If you want to be successful do what successful people do".

Having been sick plenty of times in 25 years, but have never missed a shift with the exception of passing out in the bathroom after choking on a delicious *Frito Lay Frito*, breaking the toilet seat with my head and landing in the cat box below. Never call off, someone else must cover and this strains your relationship with others and the restaurant, to quote *Peyton Manning*, "Rub some dirt on it".

I have had managers rolling on the office floor or laying down on the dinning floor with back spasms and they still hung tough. A manager tried to call off once and someone told them to come in and sit at the bar and get up only when an employee needed a swipe of their card or guest concern. I am sorry, you don't feel well, but in this business, the show must go on; 50% is better than Zero. Remember, showing up is 90% of life.

Ok, so you are on your way in for your shift, always allow for traffic and weather. Do a practice run to your store driving 100% of the speed limit to gauge the normal maximum time, now add 20 minutes to that. Would you rather sit in the parking lot or be warned or written up and be laughed at by your co-workers about your punctuality?

When approaching the building and entering the parking lot, look for trash, R.M. that needs done, landscaping and of course, bad people who want to do bad things to you and your livelihood. Before you ever enter the building you should have some goals set for the day, like becoming "King of the World", make sure your restaurant does not become like the ill-fated Titanic, remember I've hit that Iceberg twelve times.

Ah, now you are inside remember all this applies whatever shift you work. How does it look, smell, feel and even what does it sound like, ok you don't have to kiss the floor like they do at the Indy 500 row of bricks at the finish line. I have walked into floods, alarms, fires, sewer gas, broken heat or A.C., choking patrons and even an employee having an epileptic seizure passed out on the kitchen line that no one had noticed. Hey, someone call 911!

Ok, after saying Hi to everyone and making it to the office; read the manager's log book, check e-mail, talk with another manager, if possible, to see what the shift has been like or do you need to start sending out your resume again? Start implementing your plan to get promoted or making a fortune like Austin Powers "Gold Member". Do a checklist; there is always one of those. Set up your shift so you can depart on time just to do it again, but not the same the next day. Make a vow to yourself to always better the restaurant each day in a noticeable way. Cleaning, organizing, employee morale building, guest unexpected personal touches are some ways to name a few. Document these for your boss and for yourself; remember your self development should never be placed on the back burner. Remember another quote I use: "The more you know, the less stress you have".

This business can eat you alive, I've seen it from managers turning in their keys at their first day out of training or the more contemporary, a text message saying they are done, "hasta la vista"! Be more productive than your employees; a hard working reputation is favorable with everyone, but know how and when to pass the *kooky* monkey on your back everyday. My motto is I don't take monkeys, I give them, and this is a sign of an effective delegator. Try not to take too many short cuts. Hey, I'm a realist; I don't always use the side walks. Remember always, the company pays you to implement their policies and procedures, if you do this how can you lose?

It's very hard to manage people if you get involved with them on a personal level. I know you signed that six page security and procedures document again this year, but these companies are easy targets for big lawsuits and we don't want our paychecks to shrink or stop being direct deposited at all. Remember you are paid salary, that's 365 days a year, 24/7 or only 50-60 hours a week, the industry's norm.

Your daily assignments would not be complete if you were not asked to do more work, conference calls, off premise activities, for the good of you and your company. Hey, if it were easy, everyone would do it.

The guest is the number one reason you even have a job to pay your student loans or one bedroom place at "In Town Suites"; they better be forefront in your mind. The answer is "yes", what's the question or the guest may not always be right, but they are always the guest. Remember this when you look at your next 401k statement or gush at the high performing level your company's stock is listed.

For most of us in the industry, there are two schools of thought, you must temperate both with your own personal culture. It's about making personal money and it's about having a servant's heart. You serve two masters everyday and no, it's not your boss who gets drunk after his shift and sits in the bar and has sex with his wife in the women's room, yes this happened; it is the Guest and the employee.

In order to succeed, you have to have more guests than you did last year. This does not apply to your staff. You want to keep them month after month, year after year, creating as little turnover as possible, unless you like having orientation on a Saturday morning or on the fly because you need a dishwasher for dinner. My personal approach to staff is if they say jump, don't ask "how high". Don't be sarcastic or intimidating. Be thankful they want to communicate with you. Remember they are extensions of you in your business; you need to know what is going on with your staff, guests and others who come in contact with them. I have always strived to have an enjoyable fun atmosphere free from harassment and stress as much as possible. Taking it upon myself to deliver Christmas presents to the whole staff, have food buffets on big holidays when they don't or can't take a break. Through pizza party or candy sugar high moment just to say thank you for their service. This way it is all inclusive from front of the house to back of the house. Recognizing people on their birthday or work anniversary is another great way to build employee loyalty. I want to thank all of the great people I have worked with over these years, if you recognize your story; it was done with great affection and a non-malicious intent. People are truly this industry's greatest asset;

they are truly number 1 in my book. The employees were the first one in the building setting it up for their own journey before the first guest ever sets foot in the door. Bravo!

It's a not so perfect day we have to close down because our hot water heater went out. I've seen this happen over five times in 25 years. The successful restaurant will have a great relationship with its vendors and maintenance companies. A great preventative maintenance plan may stop you from pulling your hair out on a busy shift. Let's face it, you're too busy running your restaurant to change the A.C. Roof top unit filters, clean condensers, change belts or pulleys on your exhaust hood system. I will recognize one vendor for their rescue mission after a local tornado knocked out the power and leveled the hotel across the street. We were done for the day and with no power we were leaving the building as a team when a reefer truck pulled up for our use, to save our fiscal month. With flashlights in hand, in the darkest environment I have ever seen, we proceeded to wheel out the entire freezer and cooler on dollies or hand trucks. Hey, it only took three more hours, but seriously that vendor saved the day and no charge was applied for the reefer usage; not even for the fuel. Thanks so much. Washing dishes in these high volume restaurants is almost impossible with out a dish machine, but I have done it at least three times. Thanks to our vendor relationship, they fix those problems quickly 24/7; all it takes is a phone call.

I remember having to cook ribs for another unit because their oven was down. I've had to ice down product every 3 hours just to keep the food out of the temperature danger zone, 40-140 degrees, when a cooler was not working properly.

Thinking outside the box becomes routine for a restaurant manager. Hey Jim, 86 fried fish and chips a staple in our restaurant. I think not, it is time for Restaurant Man or Woman that is P.C. I raced to thaw the frozen cod and hand cutting to order, I cut my left thumb right where the joint bends; definitely needs stitches, but NO, the show must go on and no, my blood did not mingle with the frozen white fish. This does bring up managers comparing battle scars over the years, like *Mel Gibson* and *Rene Russo* comparing bullet wounds in *Lethal Weapon 3*.

Restaurants were never said to be the safest environments, "Hot, behind you".

You can't just open up your business before someone says you can, like the health inspector or excise police, if alcohol is served, and your state and federal tax man. My rule of thumb with inspections is that same old cliché. The answer is yes, what's the question. But don't cut off your nose to spite your face. Don't volunteer information; just be honest when answering theirs.

And you thought all you did is walk around with a clip board and tell others to jump through your hoops. Wrong answer, Buckwheat. This is a hands-on business. I've bussed more tables, washed more dishes and taken out more garbage than any grandma cafeteria worker has ever dreamed about. I am always the highest paid dishwasher in the city.

In each of the ten corporate restaurants I have worked for they gave me a stack of books, papers, tests, policies and procedures that you could get a nosebleed if you stood on top of the required reading and information that must be committed to memory. My best advice know its coming, jump in and read and always be a day ahead of your trainer. Otherwise I hope you can swim with out a life preserver. Hey, the great thing is they all have similar components. Serve safe is over 360 pages with tests completed online. As raunchy as it is, the movie *Waiting* actually depicted a corporate restaurant environment on acid. But still, a must watch for all hospitality people. The expectation is you learn all positions in the restaurant so you can jump in and be the net if your employees need help or don't show up. So you better be good at it and take your training seriously. You only get one chance and then it's off to the daily grind of shift management.

Avalanche

Trapped by snow in my parking lot, my poor Dodge Neon was a trooper; getting to work just before they closed the highway, when no other manager could get to work. I can't miss work, I can't miss work. We only did eight guests that day and eleven the next day, I slept one night in the restaurant and one night at the hotel next door.

Try to Keep it Fun

Practical jokes have been around since man first yelled Godzillaaa!; in the cave, back in the day. The pickle spear in the apron was my favorite. The victim would not feel it right away and eventually their fingers would gush into the pickle as they reached inside their apron pockets. Hey, you are seated a party of 8 with six high chairs or who dressed the store trophy to look like Neil Armstrong on the moon, covered in aluminum foil, carving food to look like male and female anatomy is always a favorite past time. Apron check: if I had a dollar for every time another server untied the other server's apron, I could retire. If you don't have fun; what's the point?

Employees Who are MIA

Over the years staffing each day has been a real challenge. The reasons for calling off with little or no notice varies: I'm sick, I have a flat tire, my car won't start, I forgot my shoes, I have a test, I am snowed in, my neighborhood is flooded, my grandmother is sick, had a heart attack or just died. My friend is in a coma, I forgot I had to work; I have even had someone die on the way to work. I have only missed work one time in 25 years; I was watching T.V. , eating Fritos and got choked. I went into the bathroom and literally passed out broke the toilet seat with my head and my head went into the cat litter box. The ambulance driver told me this qualified me for a day off.

Employee Down; Call 911

Seeing blood, burns and epileptic fits has qualified me as a first aid aficionado. I've had employees cut themselves, boil their skin off with and iced tea brewing basket as they pulled it out of the machine before brewing. I even turned into Restaurant Man, saving my manager who was trapped in the restaurants' elevator for over 45 minutes. No, I'm not from Krypton.

You Must be a Member to Come Inside

How much is that raccoon in the ceiling? Yes, one even gnawed through some soda lines, spraying syrup down through the ceiling on guests who were enjoying their dinner. Spiders invaded our lakeside patio one night created webs over the twenty tables on the deck. There was probably over 50 spiders, which were cleared out by our pest service the next day. I have had rats, mice and ants move in with me at work from time to time. In Florida, they don't call them roaches; they are called Palmetto bugs. I am quite sure anyone who saw these crawling across their dinner table, it was a roach by any other name. I even have had Canadian Geese nest in my flower beds, hissing at my patrons as they

harmlessly tried to make their way to the front door. Has anyone seen my 22?

I Feel Like AAA

At my first job interview out of college, a budding Italian Bistro, I locked my keys in the car. This was an hour drive from my house. I finally broke down and called my father, but as he was pulling up, the cook had heard of my dilemma and brought out his handy-dandy coat hanger; thus unlocking my door on my 1979 Chevy Impala. I proceeded to use this newly acquired skill to help many of my patrons unlock their car doors, changing flat tires, duck taping windows after break-ins and jumping car batteries to get my guest home safely; was now routine.

The Five Worst Shifts

We all do it, we tell our comrades in arms about our personal restaurant horror stories and often say this was in my top five worst shifts ever. Well, here it goes; hope you never have to share my pain.

In hind sight, what was I thinking? A party of 300 split in two seating times, an hour apart; that's 150 then after they depart, an hour later, the other 150 show. My first mistake was thinking we could ever do this at all, along with regular business. We had the seats; it was a limited large party menu. So far, so good. The first party of 150 was late by one hour. This just ate up all of my cleanup time before the next party was to arrive. The first group received their food in fine fashion. Man, I'm a great restaurateur, NOT! They were still talking and paying bills when the other 150 guests showed up. No where to sit and demanding service, I made sure to bring plenty of nails for the cross that were about to put me on. Tables slowly were getting up and the staff confused, dazed and tazed, to say the least. People started sitting at dirty tables demanding service. Knowing I could not do it all, I tried to remain the rock in the restaurant and assured everyone we can get through this, even though I was starting to waiver in my own mind. I ran around trying to help out in all areas. Remembering a quote from a manager that I often use, "this is just one of 365 days a year and we lock the doors at 10:00". This phrase has saved me and others more times than you will know. With the rest seated and fed sporadically, yes I did have to buy a lot of meals. We did open up the next day for business as usual.

After assuming command at this store after one month it was time for my first holiday, Memorial Day. How fitting as I felt like it was my funeral for me and my business. In a busy lunch environment, I ended up with 1 bartender, 1 server and 1 host as for the rest of the FOH staff, they got May Racing-itis. Each person was running six tables; their limit. We began our false wait for the next 3 hours. With me perched at the door each time a new patron entered our Italian Eatery, I would give them the stone cold truth about staffing levels and not guaranteeing seating time, looks like no breadsticks for them today. A month later, my store was given its' eulogy and like a phoenix from the flames, I was reborn in a new restaurant.

Why do I always get stuck with these shifts, well that's what all of us feel like any way. In fact, it happens to all hospitality heroes. I hear the lunch bell ringing again, only seafood is on the bill of fare for lunch today. This time the understaffed monster struck again. Only the bartender showed up, but was ready to take on the world like "Kick Ass". He literally ran 18 tables at once as I kept seating and running his food. I printed his guest checks and bussed his tables knowing I could make it alone until the 3:00 manager came in. It's true, he made a small fortune that day, but my nerves and body paid the price. You tell yourself, if you can make it through this, you can make it through anything.

It was time to celebrate Mom's Day in my new store. Too bad the best cook went back to Mexico, a week after I got there. This is a regular occurrence in our industry. They make their money here and return to the old sod as Aztec warriors with sacks of gold. But hey, this was not my first rodeo at least I have three experienced controllers of the kitchen. Well, at lest I have three warm bodies, anyway. Beginning at 1:00 for the next six hours all food took at least 1 hour to come out of the kitchen arena. My poor boss was stuck at the door till the end of time, buying mom's forgiveness and apologizing to every exasperated Dad, Son and Daughter who brought them here. One cook gave his notice while the other would be transferred out to a new store opening a month later. Happy to say, the store was rebuilt with longevity and capability and had the lowest turnover and fewest guest complaints in the region, last I checked.

The business runs on a cycle. You're busier one year and you're staffed better one year. Hey, you're just plain happier some years than other years. That's probably why I have been loyal to the industry for which I gave up 4 years of my life to be all I could be and to stare at the framed degree on the wall.

Drum roll please; the top of the five worst shifts in my career was at this Mexican eatery. Let me set the stage for you. I am El Capitan at this National Bistro. It is Saturday night and no hostess or busser has graced me with their presence. Plus the absence of all intoxicating libation concoctions mixologists has left a void in my cantina. Hey, the Margaritas still have to tango their way out to the tables. I am truly sorry the upstairs bar is closed tonight due to mechanical difficulties; a familiar lie to cover for having no bartenders' present again. By the way, as I said to the Assistant Manager on Duty, you're in the service bar tonight. He agreed with almost a sign of relief, for I was to be the one and only front man for the busiest night of the week. I did have three servers to share my pain though. I proceeded to go on a false wait for the next three hours seating100% of the guests, bussing 100% of the tables and coordinating all the carry-out business. Wish I could have said the carry-out station was broken. I only lost 3 tables to the wait and bought no meals that night due to poor service. I truly learned what it means to be the rock in the restaurant.

The Five Best Shifts

Ok, so I've got you scared and you want the name of that truck driving school, but that was only 5 days out of 9,125 days or 25 years. There have been plenty of good days as well. In similar fashion here I go, I'm in the retail business or at least this restaurant, "Got T-shirts"? The city's first FFA Convention, that's right FFA, not future farmers of America, I would soon find out. These kids in blue coats are the most polite and understanding patrons, (they must've read my book), love any kind of t-shirt, keychain and bumper stickers from this place they can get their state-represented hands on. Over the weekend of their visit, I personally rang up the store record twice for retail sales, establishing on all time store record in its' wake. I actually had fun doing this. Thinking to myself, maybe a Wal-mart checker or two could take a few pointers from this retail rock star. My boss was across the way and he gave me a silent nod to keep selling, even though I was the M.O.D. He later admitted that I was the only person in the store with the disposition and capability to handle the volume.

Having been on many Management conference trips, this one sticks out in my mind; the beautiful Mirage in Las Vegas, Nevada. Even though I only won $176 within the second pull of the Gilligan's Island one arm bandit, I was about to have an action-packed day, way different than the usual required corporate restaurant shift. From start to finish, the food was amazing, served by at least 50 servers, in a great banquet room. The message was equally impressive. Just knowing it was okay to be working just for the money was a huge revelation in restaurant reality. Never judge a book by its cover, just like this one; I'm sure it created some curiosity to the contents with in. Roy Firestone was my diamond in the rough. I had seen Roy on ESPN doing sports interviews and even saw him on the silver screen as he made Rod Tidwell cry in "Jerry McGuire". But in the middle of our banquet dinner, he gave a poetic American account of his own experiences through the medium of song. That's right; he brought the whole room to tears with the smooth golden pipes of his. I'll never underestimate anyone ever again. Having heard from a man that climbed Mt. Everest after surviving cancer and active Blue-Angel pilots and their daring teamwork maneuvers. The day was still not over; the man of 1000 voices was to be the last American Idol standing. He was the late Danny Ganns and he was the peace de resistance. Funny, talented, everything I enjoyed and wanted to do when I was seven years old. Well, I sing and dance, sing Christmas carols in summer for laughs and pretend to be the most hospitable person in the restaurant on a daily basis. Hey, I could be Danny Ganns. I think I'll just stick to cutting rib eyes and fresh salmon.

The President is Coming

No stranger to Presidential treatment, I have had three different Presidents visit me on these different shifts unannounced. Surprising even me, I was doing the right thing at the right time and in the right place all three times. The Gods are obviously smiling on me.

President number one walked through this American Bistro in the Sunshine State; I even recognized his locks of red when we made eye contact. He walked around the kitchen and the front, while he was distracted; I called my boss at home and the Area Director to tell them the good news. They were also shocked since the company was based out of Tennessee. If that was not enough, he came in again six months later Heck, we were old pals by now. I can't believe I was the manager on duty, passed inspection again. To be honest, the next visit became routine as the President lived nearby to the restaurant. So the red-carpet was always out.

However the next commander-in-chief to come a calling was quite substantial. He was the new President elect and was on a fact finding mission. He wanted to rub elbows with the common folk. Like one of the G.M's, me, of this 60 unit chain. He was the man, though, having been responsible for another chains domination growth and presence in today's pop culture, I have never seen a company president again in one of my units to date.

Step right up to the podium; it's time to receive the Golden Eagle Award for the 2nd straight year. After a visit from a regional vice president; he told me after an inspection that I was the only one trying to follow the basic corporate directives. With P+L numbers to boot, he said he was going to recommend me for this years' Golden Eagle Award. Now all this hard work is paying off.

While others question his choice, no one could deny my numbers; I took my bough and the check and life was now all sunshine and rainbows.

Ta Da! The one you have been waiting for; that's right, this one is the number one shift. The one I remember most and the one that still shapes my ultimate life goals. In the sunshine state, life is laid back and casual, and yes even supposed to be fun. My mission if I decided to accept it was to create a Beach themed weekend, complete with pirate costuming for the staff. I worked about eighty hours that week, but I didn't care, it was so much fun. I lent my artistic talent to building "Jaws" like entrance to my restaurant. Brought in sand and created a luau at the salad bar area, complete with beach chairs, blankets and umbrellas. Themed the inside with skull and cross bones, even re-named some specials and had staff members dress up including the managers. This was done to drive summer business and increase employee morale. Like George Bush Jr said, "Mission Accomplished".

I believe this was the catalyst for my first real promotion; thinking outside the box, going the extra mile or securing the booty were just some clichés that came to mind. It really was a fun shift and week knowing I could make a difference in other people's enjoyment and break from the everyday.

Corporate Decisions

They say, leadership comes from the top. I wonder if the person who said, "Let's switch to New Coke", is still employed. Two decisions stick out to me over the last 25 years along that line. How do you increase your guest counts on the weekend, that's obvious, cut out 40 seats in your restaurant. At least, this is what one exec thought.

It was mandated to get rid of all tables that seat more than 4 people. Like Aladdin, he made the wish and all the little corporate genies rented construction dumpsters and threw away their large party tables as commanded as their brand new, four top tables arrived. Mind you, no real explanation was given as to why this was a well-thought out strategic move. As the weekend approached, we readied our floor plans, I am sure copy shops across the country were thrilled. Hey, why are your sales down, clamored one regional manager, by Saturday night the big leather chair realized the folly of their decision. We suffered through the next weekend as well. Having already given our eulogy to our last supper type tables, we were assured that new six top tables would be here by the 3rd weekend. Furniture makers and delivery transports must have been gushing. They finally showed up and we had only lost 20 seats. I guess this was an acceptable substitute for efforts to increase same store guest counts.

"Have a bucket of chicken, finger licken good" the colonel has never waivered on original chicken; it has always been available. The next restaurant chain decided to, in a monetary driven decision, substitute their after dinner mints with a new option. From the very first day, guests complained and wrote letters. They even had a plane do some writing in the sky over the sunshine state. Needless to say, with the pressure on; the company went back to providing their after dinner feel good sweets, thus decreasing their profit, but ultimately increasing guest counts. I guess, the customer is always right.

Ok, so another restaurant decided to give away its' all you can eat chicken egg rolls in an effort to foster loyal guests in numbers. However, when a store goes from 4 cases in its freezer to 75 cases, that still cost the same, but they are given away; this creates a deficit you cannot reduce. I hope Obama does have a giant freezer in D.C. putting our social security tax dollars in, only to give it all away without collecting more revenues.

Uniforms have come and gone quicker than a magician and his assistants doing the quick change trick behind a falling curtain. Fresh pasta has gone by the wayside. Green onions may never recover after an FBI outbreak buried a Mexican chain. Can you say turn over, I've seen more managers come and go that could roster an NFL team a time or two. Hey, I'm sure I'm in that statistic. How about getting rid of an entire company so they could have a kick ass pool in down town Las Vegas, Only Joe would know.

The Age of Technology

Going back to the Stone Age, as my kids would say, my calculator was my computer, my cell phone was in the lobby by the bathroom; that only took quarters. People had to check their credit card statements at the End of month to see if there was an error in billing by the restaurant. I have worked with a lot of diverse equipment though, grills, proofers, dish machines, alto shams, steam stables, salamanders, bun toasters, sauté stations, steamers, walk in coolers, walk in freezers, dipper wells, microwave ovens, fryers, microphones, draft beer pulls, shrimp deveiners, automatic shrimp deveiners, chef's knives, boning knives, paring knives, meat cleavers, food mallets, serrated knives, cutting boards, salad bins, salad crispers, salad spinners, lettuce cutters, dicers, slicers, wedgers, herb cutters, lobster shears, convection ovens, cheese melters, pasta cookers, pizza ovens, tilt skillets, steam jacketed kettles, bag sealers, red buckets, glass buckets, wok stations, B.I.B stations, hotel pans, perforated pans, spoons, ladles, spoodles, buffalo choppers, vertical mixers, blenders, post blenders, burr blenders, rib pans, ticket less video screens, frozen drink machines, oyster knives, oyster spliters, breading stations, breading sifters, drip pans, wine openers, meat skewers, monkey dishes, rarebits, bullets, ramekins, soufflé cups, crocks, gratin dishes, prime rib ovens, hot drawers, cold drawers, reach in pass through, heat lamps, carving stations, buffet lines, plate dollies, crab crackers, p.o.s stations, exhaust hoods, ice paddles, thermometers, biotherms, char broilers, Cuban sandwich makers, waffle irons, hot boxes, booster heaters, hand soap dispensers, roll towel dispensers, glove holders, hand sanitizer dispensers, bar guns, margarita machines, muddlers, strainers, mixing tins, 3 compartment sinks, bar brushes, glass washers, keg dollies, pour spouts, store-N-pours, mixing spoons, two way radios, head sets, pagers, electronic seating systems, C.D. players, dance machines, music systems, bus tubs, highchairs, trays and the most important piece of equipment is the cash register.

Are you ready for Some Training?

Jim, you're going to be in training for the next six months. Having never served a day in my life, having never seen a bottle of booze, except a bottle of Early Times in my old man's liquor cabinet and cooked only chicken and burgers in the quick service eatery; I was about to become like Sponge Bob Squarepants in Sandy the Squirrel's under water dome. Or stating it differently, I was a sponge about to receive a drink for the first time. They gave me a stack of station training manuals, test booklets, mission statements, menus and progress tracking sheets. Bare in mind, there were no computers and limited videos. The expectation for all my restaurants was to start the M.I.T. in the kitchen. Prepping all food items in a few days and checking off the ominous prep sheets as you go. Next it is off to the line, where you really do become like Sponge Bob, that's right, it is to the fry/salad side, then the sauté, grill and line Q.B. or expo. As you round home, you go to the alley and expedite the finished plates, being the last person to see the food. Make sure to call for a server to run the food, "hot food go, you can't say no." The expeditor is the main kitchen role for most kitchens managers, after spending five weeks in the kitchen; you are shuffled off to the FOH. Host training, bussing tables and hey, maybe that all important toilet cleaner position. As you brush the bowls, you reminisce about your night in the dish tank when the E.O.N pots, pans, plates, and the like would not stop coming. You truly were the highest paid dishwasher in the city. Now it's time to go to the dark side. It's your turn to be a server. You have to memorize the entire menu and alcoholic offerings. Remember if they are a percentage tipper, the bigger the check, the more money you make. My first solo table was a two-top; the trainer gave me my wings. The male guest ordered chicken cordon bleu and stuffed flounder for his wife. I remember his order now but turned it in wrong to the kitchen that fateful day. It's amazing I stayed in this business for 25 years and counting. Now it was the bartender's time to have their way with me. Ok, you need to memorize all these bottles and learn how to make a Cuba Libra, like *Tom Cruise* in *Cocktail*. In the future, I would coach servers to know at least two liquors, for each base liquor so they can up-sell. To quote Mr. Crabs "I want me money"! Now it's time to play manager, now that you have learned all the restaurants basic positions. You are clearly eye-balling that M.I.T conference, in a far away state, that all managers eventually attend; just one of the many, mind you.

You will learn to open, close and work a mid shift. Where did I put that checklist? You will do daily, weekly and monthly orders and inventories. By the end of one of these training programs, if you did your daily homework, played jeopardy with the menu, beer, liquor and wine; you might just get a set of keys. The market is truly competitive these days and in an effort to keep costs down and have reduced turnover; fear the word P.F.W (Promote from Within), no college degree required. I've worked with great managers and not so great ones. Believe you me; I could care less who has a degree in this stuff, as long as I know when the store is getting bum rushed , they've got my back.

It's Time to Advertise How Great You Are

I doubt you'll ever be on TV. But who knows, remember I sang about my restaurant on stage for an audience of 500 potential patrons. Donating restaurant food to a radio station that was promoting our open interview event was my first on air blunder; I was more worried about the DJ getting my name right than the event itself. Stupid is as stupid does, I guess you could say. Off premise events are important to your business and remind you of why you like working in the restaurant everyday. I've appeared at my University, the greatest race track in America, done dozens of complementary cuisine calls on unexpecting businesses, participated in recurring rib fests in the great Midwest and fed over 500 at a high school charity event. Aside from cooking, transporting, setting up, serving, and clean up, your bosses are going to want pictures, summaries and hey, maybe even a book on about why they paid you not to work in their restaurant that day. There is never a week; month or year that goes by, that someone does not want a free meal from your establishment. That's right, donation requests are a routine interruption in your business day. I even had the beggars complain about the donation amount and refuse the restaurant's offering; stating that the restaurant must need it more than they do. Themed weekends, holidays, and just a break from the everyday, help your guests to stand out from all the rest; a sound validation to why you are still on the payroll. Ok, I was on TV once, delivering a hot steaming plate of crab to my boss who had the spotlight. This was my five forgettable seconds of fame. I guess singing, television star and musical personal appearances by moi, is one way to put my advertising stamp on this flavor of the year's business.

A Reminder about my College Days

It's 7:30 a.m. and I am in my first University class, Starbucks has not even swept across the county yet, and I was about to learn about Quantity Food Sanitation. If you want to be successful and prepare yourself for the real world, well, not reading this book does not do you any favors, but seriously, I hear students say this all the time, me included. This school of the future bread winners club did not prepare me for the real world. Help Me! Help You! Take a course in public speaking. Learn to be timely and organized with your school's degree demands. Read excerpts on proper interviewing, practice in the mirror making sure to smile. Remember you are going to be on the hospitality stage 24/7, 365. That's right; you represent your company everyday that you are employed by them. So watch out for the late night parties, or trips to the local men's club; that was recently in the paper for a professional Athletes's atrocious behavior with his Smith and Wesson.

Sometimes, it's hard to see the value at your school as you're going through March of Madness. It's truly about diversity and how you fit in to the human chess board. Grades are important, but No one ever asked me what grade I got in the Hospitality Law; it was a "B". Maybe if I got an A, I would not have been fined by EEOC for improper documentation for the termination of a Prep Cook; a mistake I'll never made again. I use Hospitality Accounting every day when I wash dishes, as suggested by the professor. This saves labor and creates less turnover and demonstrates to others that I'm willing to get my hands dirty, thus going to the bottom line, short term and long term. Thanks, professor, I think. My hands are all white and pruney from the dish sprayer; *Palmolive*, come to my rescue! So, you had to participate in a mock restaurant; I know I did. FOH and BOH with International Flare "007" would have been proud. You really are like "M" directing all of the resources and high level players. Being calm under pressure is a prerequisite for this type of organization. It's like you being critiqued from your professors and peers everyday. They are just waiting for you to slip up. You got to get a handle on the brain mouth thing to earn respect and be taken seriously. Remember you can't run the race for your team only give them direction to the finish line. In other words, you have to delegate without fear. Make it a game: see how many productive necessary hoops you can make people jump through everyday. Think of yourself like Sonic the Hedgehog Collecting those little golden rings and at the end of the month, you get a pot of gold at the bottom of your profit and loss statement.

Hey, school is not all work and no play; this makes you an unsuccessful multi-tasker. That's right, I made it a point to participate in sports, clubs, on campus health and safety presenter and I even graced the stage as a stage hand for Frankenstein.

Employers like an applicant with diversity; if you live off campus, you better have hobbies and interests that make you interesting. At least 10 times, over a three week interview process that I went through yielded an offer. It is not always about the money, however. I once turned down a job offer this year that was going to pay me fat cash, but I turned them down because I could not see me in that environment.

My first job was selected because they had the best training program; this was a sound choice in my opinion. Since fast food was all I had to reference, it only made sense to take it slow and only slip into the restaurants waters, instead of doing a cannonball. I guess it is okay to say, I made a whopping $17,500 a year, thanks to my Alma Mater. Don't worry the government did raise the minimum wage a couple years ago, ok, are you ready for the secrets of the universe, everything is negotiable. That's right; you don't have to settle for the first offer you get. Tips for making a good living are worth the price of this book alone. Ask around the industry, talk with some managers, look at internet wage averages and ask for more than you are willing to settle for with in reason. Recruiters want to get you as cheap as they can. My motto in college was never pay full price for anything. I always used coupons at Dominos or Arby's 5-for-5 deal. Remember all car dealers negotiate the price, furniture stores, electronics and jewelry as well as contractors. Don't pay full price because you don't want to skip the stress that comes with standing your ground. I bought an all-in-one computer from Best Buy for only $ 449.00; a savings of $ 50.00 off the floor model with same as brand new warranty.

Training M.I.T.s

Now that you are all colleged up, it's time to start over at the bottom as a M.I.T. That's right, manager in training. Pick your company wisely, but know what I said earlier still applies. I always try to give the new recruit a positive beginning. Hey, I might work with them one day. Connecting and engaging, I tell them they will probably want to quit in the next two weeks. But this feeling will soon pass. You see, you know nothing and no one and everyone is always attempting to dig out what you do know. The key is listening and knowing what kind of learner you are. Are you a watcher, reflector, thinker or doer; or a combination? Make sure to keep up with your training guide and do what it says, day by day, always reading ahead and be prepared for tomorrow's lesson. Listen to your Certified Trainers and ask lots of questions. Remember, you are not there to change the world. You are there to learn how the company and ultimately, your boss want things done. So you will probably work 5 days a week, ten hours a day plus homework and home study. College gets you the degree and the interview, but the real learning begins when you start an M.I.T program. I've seen them come and go and I have trained over 30 M.I.T.s in various restaurants over the years. That's enough managers to staff a chain restaurant representation in any large city. They say there is no dumb question, only the one that is not asked. But when I asked you to memorize a computer process, recipe ingredients or steps of service, you may want to write it down cause there will be a test, and I don't want to have to embarrass you by stating the obvious.

Don't try to act like you are busy, honestly, I can see that from across the restaurant. Try to be productive, asking ok, what's next? Be on time. Again, quoting my Father, "to be on time is to be five minutes early". Many managers and M.I.T.s have gotten on my bad side over the years with their nonchalant attitude towards punctuality. Having only missed two shifts in the past 25 years and only late twice, I am consistently 10 minutes early for every shift, instilled by my father. I figure the company stills owes me 65,000 minutes or 1083 hours for responsible on-time shifts; if only to serve as an example. I will greatly accept the almost One-month salary that has accumulated in the last 25 years. In truth, people are rarely penalized in their careers for tardiness. As an example, one manager was actually promoted for being 20 minutes late almost daily for an entire year, but I wouldn't roll the dice.

Staffing: It takes All Types

Never underestimate the power of diversity. It's not who you hang out with, it's who will do the best job in the position that allows you to sleep at night. There is no room for prejudices; racism or gay bashing anymore. With the labor market shrinking, the victor of the war on employees is the one with the lowest turnover. As "Purple" has taught us, your name could be Rainbow and if you show up and do your job, nothing else should matter. I remember a gang member working in my kitchen, unfortunately, the PoPo snatched him in the middle of the shift; he was a good cook though. Sometimes, it does not work out , but don't let it form opinions or turn them away, because they are not like you. I have always been proud of my senior citizen dishwasher who worked 7 days a week, 363 days a year, opening from 9-2, that's never getting overtime. Mr. Ling was the most consistent employee that I have ever seen. This Asian man worked for us, for three years until we shut our doors. Shay Shay Nee, Mr. Ling. I've utilized special needs people to contribute to the team's success.

Our industry allows us to have these employees for certain tasks, giving them pride in their accomplishments and job fulfillment. A girl with Downs syndrome once gave me a campaign bracelet; "Spread the word to End the Word" and she stated to me that she was just a person; not a retard. I would say most kitchens in which I have worked, are Hispanic in majority. The true diversity is when we hire a Caucasian with the same work ethic and can fit in with these friends from South of the Border. A charming senior from across the pond used her "Mrs. Doubtfire" like charms to seat the guest and open doors for all she could. Thank you Miss Cindi. Make sure to thank everyone daily and say hello and goodbye. Get to know each person, not just their first name; these are real flesh and blood people and they deserve your loyalty to their individuality. Celebrate your restaurant's success, but hold all of them accountable. People enjoy a well disciplined environment and they know what to expect.

A Friendless Business

I have found it hard to maintain relationships outside of my family. With such a varied schedule and jumping the broom, so to speak, I don't get to know anyone long enough. Remember, I worked at multiple units as well. The total number of restaurants in which I have worked is 26, averaging more than one restaurant per year. Some managers work in one restaurant all their lives. It just depends on the kind of person you are.

The Grass is not always Greener

Tired of my job, sick of the hours and the B.S. was never really a reason for my job hopping; more money, in my pocket, location and prestige were the real drivers, before you make the switch, you must evaluate all areas. Don't make the decision when you are angry or based on one shift and certainly, don't burn a bridge. You never know when you will end up there again needing a steady paycheck. It's obvious by now I don't have any fear starting over, this comes as your experience and Industry knowledge grows. I told you it is relatively the same where ever you go. The biggest motivator for me is the people that I work with on a daily basis; they make or break my quality of life. In other words, the grass is not always greener somewhere else.

Road to Promotion

I always did set out to become a G.M. of my own unit. I wanted my parents to be proud of me, and the degree they helped pay for was put to good use. Working my tail off for six years before someone gave me the reigns at 28 years old; this is still really young for General Manager. I would spend 12 years in this position having climbed the latter in four corporations and the fifth made an offer that I ultimately did not accept. I still act like a leader, but take the leadership direction easily from the current General Manager. I never aspired to be an Area Manager; I wanted to be home every night and be responsible for only what was in my four walls. If you want to ascend quickly on the menu for Management; reread this book; it will tell you how to get there. Just don't take shortcuts, be full of energy and have a sense of urgency and most importantly, smile and have fun!

My Goals for the Future

I'm afraid I am at the tale end of my restaurant Management career, only five or six years left in operations. Hey, a guy has to know when he can't play the kids game anymore. This industry has helped me to keep young though. I do plan to retire in Florida with my lovely wife. Hey, I might work for Mickey Mouse performing daily in the Electric Parade or working on a pleasure boat as a deck hand or maybe performing at a local dinner theater as one of the senior regulars to the delight of all the retirees. Whatever it is, I will look back on the industry spending my 401k and knowing the restaurant business made my dreams possible.

A Glimpse of the Future

What will restaurants be like in the future? You already have seen where grocery stores and Wal-mart have created Self-checkout lines and some chains have touch screen tablets on the table where you can order dessert and even pay your bill. Back to the future even showed us how cafes are in futuristic sense. I believe credit card readers may be mobile consistently tableside or you might have to swipe your card before you dine, no cash accepted. This would eliminate walkouts like I'm sure Cracker Barrel still has in droves. This will also speed up your tables' average time thus increasing business and lessoning the number of servers needed to work a section. Unfortunately, I see prices rising and portion sizes decreasing to fight our national obesity epidemic. They already started to pair restaurants together producing all types of food from a central kitchen; look for these to rise in popularity. Then you really will have to know two companies and two menus. Hey, you think they will double their pay for everyone? I think not. Being at the top of my pay grade, I will never see another base pay increase, in fact I have never received a raise in the last five years. Plan your monthly budget and spend only what you can afford and think about your long term spending needs and you will do just fine.

As Caucasians become the minority in this country the FOH staffing will change more and more, it will be like a cruise ship dining experience only more of a melting pot of human players. Who knows, one day each table might have a video screen server like "Max Headroom" and take your orders and the manager would appear electronically if you are dissatisfied. From the day of "Ray Croc" things sure have changed. Who knows what things will be like in the future, I only hope Mc Donald's French fries are still the bomb.

Closing Thoughts

As I come to the end of my novelistic journey, I hope you got a look into the industry, gained some Management perspective and walked with me in my shoes down the buffet line that is "The Buffet of Diversity". From the people that I worked with, the guests that I have served and the managers who helped keep everything with in the four walls. To quote Jim Parsons, the actor on *The Big Bang Theory*, I say "Bazinga" to all; just call me, "Purple".

The End

Acknowledgements

1. The Frankfort Times—The Prince of Pumpkins article and photograph
2. The Parsons' Family Joni ,Katie ,Amanda, and A.J.

About the Author

Jim Parsons was born in Charleston West Virginia. He grew up in Frankfort Indiana and resides in Lebanon Indiana. He has been in the restaurant business for 25 years and graduated in 1988 from Purdue University; majoring in Restaurant Management. He enjoys pumpkin carving, singing and weight lifting. He has been married to his high school sweetheart for over 25 years and has raised three children. He always likes to change things up with his daily routine, artistically speaking. Who knows what he will do next.

Jim with Scarecrow in Pumpkin Patch